Flight of the Monarch

by Emily Lesser
illustrated by Graham Smith

Harcourt
SCHOOL PUBLISHERS

Printed in China

ISBN 10: 0-15-350685-7
ISBN 13: 978-0-15-350685-7

Ordering Options
ISBN 10: 0-15-350600-8 (Grade 3 On-Level Collection)
ISBN 13: 978-0-15-350600-0 (Grade 3 On-Level Collection)
ISBN 10: 0-15-357906-4 (package of 5)
ISBN 13: 978-0-15-357906-6 (package of 5)

1 2 3 4 5 6 7 8 9 10 985 12 11 10 09 08 07 06

It is late August on the border of Canada and the United States. A monarch butterfly is getting ready to come out of its chrysalis. This monarch butterfly is different from its parents and its grandparents. It will not lay eggs right away like most female monarchs. It will also live far longer than the monarch butterflies that appeared earlier in the summer.

Before it becomes a butterfly, this insect goes through different stages. These stages take about two weeks. First, the mother butterfly lays an egg. When the egg hatches, there is a caterpillar. The caterpillar is very hungry. First, it eats the case of its egg. Then, it eats leaves from a plant called milkweed to build up fat to give it energy. It also eats milkweed to protect it from predators. Milkweed is poisonous to most animals, so they will stay away from the butterfly.

Egg

Larva (caterpillar)

When it is bigger, the caterpillar makes its chrysalis. The chrysalis hangs from the stem of the milkweed plant. The caterpillar changes in the chrysalis. Finally, a butterfly comes out of the chrysalis! It rests and waits for its wings to dry. When they dry, the monarch will be able to fly.

You may think this is normal. Any butterfly can fly. This butterfly is special, though. This monarch who arrives in late summer will make an amazing journey.

Chrysalis

Adult (butterfly)

The monarch will fly over mountains. It will avoid animals that try to eat it. It will find its way to a place thousands of miles away that it has never seen.

We do not know every detail of its coming trip. We do not know how it knows where to go. Scientists think that the monarch uses the sun to help it figure out which direction to go.

As autumn nears, shorter days and cooler weather tell the monarch it is time to go. It sets off on its long flight. Soon millions of monarchs will be in the air.

A monarch usually lives alone. On its fall trip, though, it will travel with a large group of monarchs. This group of monarchs will sip nectar from flowers along the way. Nectar gives a butterfly the energy it needs for its long trip. Sometimes the monarchs will huddle together to keep warm at night.

The monarch may fly almost two miles (3.22 km) up in the sky on its journey. It flaps its wings between five and twelve times every second. Strong winds may blow it off course. It still knows the way. Millions of these butterflies will make their way to their winter homes. If you are lucky, you may get to see a monarch on its way. In September and October, you might see it as it swoops in the sky.

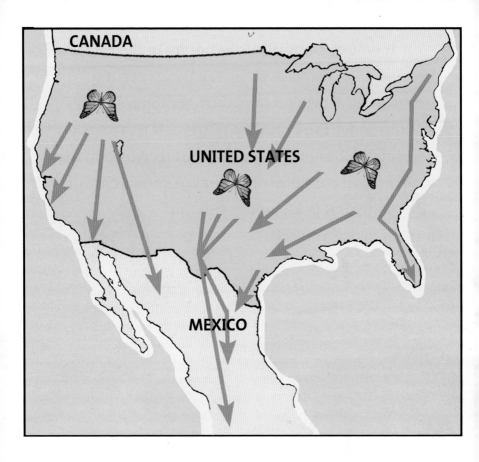

The distance to the monarch's winter grounds may be as much as three thousand miles (4,823 km). The trip may really be much longer, though. A monarch does not fly straight like birds do. Wind or weather may take the butterfly out of its way. If the wind is too strong, the monarch will wait until the wind dies down. It may go around or over forests or mountains.

A monarch butterfly does not fly in the rain because if its wings get wet, the wings are too heavy to fly. During a rainstorm, a monarch takes shelter under the branches of trees. If its wings do get wet, the butterfly must wait for its wings to dry before it can continue on its way. A monarch will also not fly if it is too hot. It will find a shady place and rest.

The journey will take about two months. Scientists that track the monarch have discovered that it can fly fifty to a hundred miles (80–160 km) a day. It is not nocturnal, so it dozes at night, and it flies during the day.

Monarchs east of the Rocky Mountains go to a special place in Mexico high up in the mountains. Many monarchs west of the Rocky Mountains go to a place in California. This place is called Pacific Grove, but most people call it Butterfly Town USA! Everything here is perfect for the butterflies. It has just the right temperature, and it also has protection from the wind.

When the monarch finally arrives at its winter home, there will be millions of other butterflies there, too. Each year the monarchs return to the same exact trees! The butterflies huddle together in the trees in an effort to keep warm. There are thousands upon thousands of them hanging on top of each other. In this way, the butterflies wait out the winter.

When spring comes, the monarch begins to move. It gets ready to set off on its journey home. The monarch will not make it all the way back home, though. It will die along the way.

Before the monarch dies, it will mate and lay its eggs. These eggs will hatch, form a chrysalis, and finally turn into butterflies. This offspring of the monarch butterfly will continue the long trip back home.

The pattern will begin again. Summer will come and go, and several sets of monarchs will live their lives. Then autumn will draw near. The last monarchs of summer will get ready for their trip.

Now monarchs face new dangers along the way. Human activity is their greatest enemy. There are not as many safe places left. Even winter resting spots are in danger because humans may cut down the trees.

A butterfly waits, its wings fluttering. It is the last monarch of summer. Soon it will be on its way.

Think Critically

1. How does the monarch butterfly know when it is time to start its trip?

2. How are the last monarchs that hatch each summer different from their parents?

3. Why don't monarch butterflies fly in the rain?

4. What might happen if the trees where the monarchs rest are cut down?

5. What do you think is the most amazing thing about the monarchs?

 Science

A Butterfly Garden Some people grow gardens especially for butterflies. Find out what kinds of plants would work well in a butterfly garden and why.

 School-Home Connection Tell friends and family members about the amazing flight of the monarch. Then talk about some of the difficulties the butterfly must experience on its long journey.

Word Count: 944 (950)